STUDY &
RESEARCH

STUDY & RESEARCH

a systematic approach
for all students

How to prepare, write, & successfully complete:

- **AN ESSAY**
- **A RESEARCH PAPER**
- **A DISSERTATION**
- **A THESIS**

Dr Roland Newman

BOOKMARQUE
PUBLISHING

First published October 1989

British Library Cataloguing in Publication Data

Newman, Roland
    Study & Research: a systematic approach for all students:
    how to prepare, write and successfully complete an essay,
    a research paper, dissertation or thesis.
    1. Higher education institutions. Students. Study techniques
    I. Title
    378'.17'02812

    ISBN 1–870519–06–X

Set in 10 on 12½ point Palatino
Typography/design by John Rose
Edited by Tom Colverson
Printed and bound by Antony Rowe Ltd · Chippenham · Wiltshire
Published by Bookmarque Publishing · Minster Lovell · Oxford

CONTENTS

SECTION *1*   **How to prepare for writing an essay,**
research paper, dissertation or thesis   11
Learning to read   12
Stages 1, 2, 3   12
Taking notes   15
Forming the structure   17
Organising notes   24

SECTION *2*   **Writing it out**   29
A first draft   30
The Introduction and Conclusion   33
Putting the facts together   35
Miscellaneous points   37

SECTION *3*   **The Structured Question Technique**   41
Phases A, B, C   45

SECTION *4*   **Aids to writing**   49
Overcoming Writer's Block   50
Word processing (additional facilities)   54

Selected References   63

The life and role of a student is a lonely, often frightening and worrisome affair. I earnestly trust that this small book will provide a few glimpses of light and some stepping stones as you commence your struggle across the bogs of ignorance and through the quicksands of over-whelming data and the sloughs of despond.

SECTION 1

HOW TO PREPARE FOR
WRITING AN ESSAY, RESEARCH PAPER,
DISSERTATION OR THESIS

1

HOW TO PREPARE FOR WRITING AN ESSAY, RESEARCH PAPER, DISSERTATION OR THESIS

It is clear that whilst discussion of the theories and methods of research and study is of great interest (especially to their tutors) what most students seem to require is some PRACTICAL guidance, particularly on how to go about selecting, delimiting and then structuring their proposed area of study or research.

Accordingly the purpose of this section is to suggest some practical ways in which you can attempt to tackle the problem of defining and then structuring your proposed work.

To raise the subject of 'learning to read' is perhaps one way of edging into this difficult problem. Apparently irrelevant at this stage, it will, I trust, become clear how it eventually links into the structure of this book.

LEARNING TO READ

By 'learning to read' I mean acquiring the technique of learning how to 'tear the heart out of books' or how to 'gut' them efficiently and quickly. You, the student, must by now be aware that you will have to work your way through a large number of books, articles and other forms of written information, and to do this you must acquire the technique of dealing efficiently with the masses of information which you will almost certainly accumulate.

There are a number of techniques available and an even greater number of publications on increasing reading and comprehension speed. Assuming that your reading speed is adequate, these techniques fall into a basic pattern as follows:

STAGE 1

Erase from your mind any previous pattern of reading that required you to start at the beginning and read through the book or article to the end. Instead, try to gain some quick impression of what the book is about; what question or questions the author is trying to answer; how the book is structured; and whether, in fact, the questions tackled and the answers put forward are relevant to your needs. Do this by looking at the 'blurb' on the cover or jacket, the preface (if any), the list of contents and glancing quickly through the index. Try then to gain an overall impression of the book and its structure. But, above all, try to formulate in your mind what question or questions the author is trying to answer, and assess their relevance to your own area of study or research.

STAGE 2

Assuming that you have decided that the book or article is relevant, then you must try to formulate, as clearly as possible, the questions that you believe to be answered in it. Perhaps even pause and write them down. Having formulated these questions then move on to the next stage. I must emphasise that the formulation of questions plays a vital part in this technique. You simply can no longer afford to read aimlessly through a book but must have decided at this stage what information you want from it, and you must adopt an active and analytical attitude if this technique is to be successful.

STAGE 3

Once you have formulated the main question or questions, you must now search through the book for the answers to these questions. Already from your examination in Stage 1 you will have some idea where to look for these answers. You are thus now searching for the parts of the book where the questions that are of interest to you have been dealt with. When you have located these questions you must then look for the answers or conclusions that the author has put forward, and above all find out (if you can!) how he/she arrives at them. You will also be seeking for the arguments and evidence put forward to support these views and you will be attempting to assess the validity of the evidence and the structure of argument utilising such evidence. In other words what you will be learning to do is to fillet out the backbone of the author's work and lay bare the structure of questions, argument and evidence leading to the answer, argument or case the author is trying to make out.

What you will be leaving out are the analogies (and I shall write more about the dangers of analogies in later sections), the anecdotes, the descriptive and supporting paragraphs, and, of course, the great deal of additional writing that the author must put in to balance and make the work more palatable. But take warning – when you apply this technique you may well be in for some surprises. Often you will find a conclusion interposed in a few words in the earlier paragraphs of a chapter and you may eventually find the supporting argument and evidence at the end of the chapter or even in later chapters. Of course, there are cases where you will find unsupported conclusions or even no argument or evidence at all, and occasionally there will be instances when there is no conclusion either!

'How reductionist, how philistine, how dreary!' you may say. You take a beautifully written book, perhaps tastefully illustrated and a real work of art, and you attempt to reduce it to its bare bones. I can only agree: it is appalling but from your point of view unless you are to quote massive chunks of the book concerned, you have to try to tease out the essence of the book, and above all you must do it quickly. Later, when you have the time and inclination, you can go back and savour the literary delights of the author's ability, but for the moment you must move on quickly to the next stage.

STAGE 4

Assuming that by now you have extracted the essential information from the book or article concerned, you must now get it into note form. The commonest method is to use small filing cards, and the essential feature is to put the minimum of information on each card. I shall return to discuss this method later in this section.

TAKING NOTES

For the moment the essential requirement is that, except for quotations, you must try to avoid taking notes direct from the book or article concerned. First, because for note-taking you must use your own active vocabulary and not the author's, for it is generally agreed that each individual has an active vocabulary – one he/she uses in speaking or writing – and a passive vocabulary – the one used in reading and understanding another person's work. Normally the individual's passive vocabulary is much larger than his/her active vocabulary. If you doubt that nearly all individuals do have quite differing active and passive vocabularies, you should try reading out to a number of friends a reasonably complicated but understandable article and then ask them to write out a summary of that article. Leaving aside the complexities of individual interpretations, inert biases and varying ideologies, the variation in the vocabularies used is often quite astounding. It is vitally important to use the active vocabulary in note-taking, because it helps to ensure that you have a reasonably full grasp of the meaning of the information concerned; it possibly assists in laying down a better memory trace in the brain and finally when you come to re-read and synthesise the notes, your personal active vocabulary is more easily comprehensible and recognisable. In addition, if you do not attempt to turn the author's words into your own active vocabulary, you invariably find that after a short while, you are blindly and boringly copying out great masses of information direct from the book or article concerned. How to transform what one has read into an active vocabulary note form varies from individual to individual, but certainly one method is to physically close the book and turn away from it before attempting to write out the relevant notes. This system, you will discover, also acts as a check, for often what you think has been comprehended accurately turns out to be quite inaccurate and unstructured when you try to write it out in note form.

Let us now turn again to the form in which to accumulate notes. Some systems recommend filing cards, others pieces of note paper – but the essential feature is that each card or piece of paper must contain only ONE idea or ONE fact or ONE question. The reason for this apparently wasteful procedure is that at this stage you cannot be certain in which part of your structure of research, extended study or essay, this ONE piece of information will be used.

Indeed, you may not even be certain it will be used at all. The system then depends upon the accumulation of facts, ideas, quotations and arguments – each of which will be on separate cards or pieces of paper – and this means that each of them can be slotted into separate parts of the structure of the work which you may have, at this stage, roughly in mind. If subsequently the structure is changed it is not too difficult to sift through and replace the cards etc., into the new structure as each card or piece of paper will contain only one item. However, if more than one item is contained on the card or piece of paper, and any restructuring is found necessary, then difficulties will arise as one fact or item may 'belong' to one part of the structure and the other item(s) on the same card or slip may 'belong' elsewhere. One final point before we turn to the structure itself. Great pains must be taken to ensure that the source of the information, idea, quotation or argument is clearly and accurately shown on each card or piece of paper. It is essential that each note, fact, idea or quotation etc. can later be accurately traced back to its origin or source!

FORMING THE STRUCTURE

Now let us turn again to the formulation of the structure: we will start with a rather simpler essay structure, though when you understand the system you will see that the underlying principles are always identical even with complex subjects over a wide range of disciplines. You will remember that when I discussed reading techniques earlier in this section, the premise which I put forward was that each book or article (other than fiction) is written with the intention of answering a question or series of questions. One method therefore of setting about formulating a structure is to try to set out the question or questions that, for example, an essay, extended or otherwise, is trying to answer.

Let us take the example given overleaf.

AN EXAMPLE

You, the student, are set a task of writing an essay about a building of your choice dealing with the history – the architectural history, or the social and economic history, of the building concerned – though you should clearly understand that this technique can be applied to any essay or research subject! The object is, as quickly as possible, to try to 'break in' to the subject by setting out a series of questions which will make the subject more manageable and handleable, and replace the amorphous fog which generally tends to surround it at this stage.

The questions can be set out under the various headings that may occur to you, viz:

The Building itself

Who was the client?
Why was it built?
What materials were used?
What was the degree of sophistication of services?
What constructional techniques were used?
Who were the subsequent owners?
Why did the ownership change?
What additions/alterations were made, and why?
Did these match the original style?

The Site

How was it chosen?
What was its relationship to its surroundings?

The Architect

Who was the architect?
Where/how was he trained?
What were his intentions?
Were they achieved?
How does his/her work fit into the architectural thought and ideas prevalent at that time?
What were the architectural fashions of that time?

The Builders
Who built it?
What building techniques were used?
Where did the labour come from?
What sort of men made up the labour force?

The Local Community
Did the building play a part in local affairs
a) on completion?   b) subsequently?
What was the history of the local community?
Has the local community changed economically or socially?

The Owner
a) What part did he play in local, county or national affairs?
   What was his source of wealth?
   Was his wealth connected with a particular economic factor?
   Has this economic factor changed? Why? How?
   What were the subsequent owners?
b) What sort of social life did he (they) have?
   What sort of domestic/private life did he/they have?
   What status symbols were indulged?

The National Factors
What were the economic, religious and political characteristics of
   the nation at the time the house was built?
Were the local community or the owner directly connected with a
   particular economic factor?
Have these changed? How?

Can you now see how your initial problem has been trans-
formed? Whereas earlier you were uncertain of how to proceed
you are now confronted with a totally different problem of having
a multitude of choices. Your problem now is to decide which of
the questions you will attempt to answer.

In addition, from past experience, it is clear to me that most
students, confronted by such a list of questions connected with
the subject they are considering, are soon able to expand and

amplify the list of questions and even to change the series of headings.

Well, in an ideal research situation it would theoretically be possible for you to explore all the research sources available and then, following your own interests, to select such questions as you think fit and put them together to form a suitable structure. In reality two factors intrude. First, the time constraint usually imposes a sharp limit on the amount of research that can be carried out, and, secondly, the sources of material available are usually of such a limited nature that you can only attempt a limited number of questions.

A working compromise at this stage is therefore to prepare the list of questions and then to devote such time as is available to seeking out and investigating the research sources available. Armed with your prepared list of questions and using the reading technique described above (though no notes should be taken at this point), you will probably discover that the questions which can then be tackled dwindle in number, dependent on the type of essay or research paper you are required to write.

You are now in a position to attempt to research more deeply into this reduced number of questions. But it is often wiser even then to search amongst these remaining questions for ones which are likely to interest and therefore motivate you. You should realise that it is possible to devote an enormous amount of time to answering even just a few of the questions concerned. For the normal student, however, with little time and scarce sources of information, it is probable that tackling between five and ten questions will usually be more than enough.

So let us recap. You started off by formulating a large number of questions, and in this way broke down the major problem posed by the subject into a series of questions or sub-problems. Then because source material was limited or not available and taking into account the time available and your own particular interests, you selected a much reduced list of questions. At this stage, I trust, the question of structure is beginning to intrude upon your mind. The final questions must clearly be of such a nature that they will fit into a pattern or structure which can form the outline of the essay. From the answer to these questions your aim must be to construct a coherent, logical pattern of ideas and argument that will form the structure or backbone of your essay or paper. Into this structure the data which you have discovered can then be fitted to 'flesh out' and support your theme, argument or thesis.

This process is difficult to describe as the combinations of the questions available are enormous. Generally speaking, however, if the questions of the architecture and the architect alone were selected (provided these met the conditions laid down as the basis of the essay) it would be reasonable to expect you to give, in the earlier part of your essay, a general description of architecture and architects at the given time. You might also wish to relate the architecture to architectural ideas and trends in Europe or elsewhere at that period. If you decided to concentrate on the technology, then again a general description of technical methods would be expected. Perhaps the owner was a famous politician or landowner, in which case some general background material on the political system or the farming system would be necessary preparation for the subsequent discussion. Although in principle it is better to avoid analogies except as literary devices, perhaps the analogy of painting a picture is not too inappropriate on this occasion.

The structure which you are seeking is the frame, and having selected the size of the canvas and the central feature you will eventually use, you have to select the correct background relative to this central feature. Clearly you must not finish up with any blank spaces, but equally your selected background must relate correctly to the detail in the main part of the picture. Let's take two examples, one at each end of the scale.

Supposing you were required to concentrate on the details of windows only in the building concerned. It would then be possible for you to give only brief details of the house and thereafter to concentrate on the windows, probably relating them to the development of windows in general.

Conversely at the other end of the scale, if the house selected was Georgian it might prove acceptable to use only the details of the chosen house and to compare and contrast it with other Georgian houses, against a background description and discussion of Georgian period architecture in general.

But two points must be kept continually in mind. First, the conditions laid down for the essay must be adhered to – otherwise all your work is wasted. If you are required to write an essay on the architectural aspects of the house – then on the whole your essay or research paper must deal with the architectural aspects. If you are required to write a social history essay, then the basic content of the essay must deal with the social history aspects of the building.

Secondly, you must take an active and critical attitude to your essay. It is not enough to assemble masses of descriptive facts and then shape these into some form of apparent structure designed to try to hide the emptiness of thought which underlies it. As the facts and ideas are accumulated they must be criticised and analysed; the evidence – implicit or explicit – of the source material provided must be considered on its merits. Throughout the whole process of material accumulation you must try to take a doubting and irreverent attitude.

In trying to adopt this critical attitude, the whole technique of question formulation plays a part. Not only must you be considering whether you have asked the right questions, but in considering the answers which you have discovered for yourself, or writers have put forward, you must try to assess the supporting evidence and arguments and decide for yourself whether they are sufficient and valid. In this way the structure can 'come alive' and the mass of facts which you have accumulated can become vital components supporting a coherent structure of argument rather than a dreary mass of descriptive material wedged into the essay in a haphazard way.

So, if we return to the stage when you are considering the final set of questions which you are attempting to answer, you must, even at this early stage, be attempting to formulate a structure of argument into which the mass of information you will shortly be accumulating can fit.

It is unusual at this early stage to have more than a vague outline of this structure and you must be prepared to change and restructure it as your work proceeds. The essential feature, though, is for you to be constantly seeking for such a structure which will allow you to build up a 'framework' of argument into which your 'bricks' of information can be neatly fitted and which supports your conclusion 'pinnacle'. To paraphrase and invert McLuhan 'the message is the argument' and the argument is the structure.

Now let us return to the reading technique described earlier, to the point where you are beginning to collect items of facts, information, quotations etc., on single cards or single slips of paper.

You will by now have assembled your list of final questions and have some glimmering of an overall structure which may well be in the form of an all-embracing and comprehensive question. At this stage you can use your question list to define areas of study that you are going to tackle. Based on the example given earlier you might use your questions to form subject areas such as:

House: When built. Architecture. Construction.

Owner: Sources of wealth. Political career.

Community: Small landowners. Based on sheep.

These subjects areas are important not only because they break down the whole subject into manageable portions, but, more important still, because they form a system of categorisation or filing as the items are collected on the cards or slips of paper.

ORGANISING NOTES

It is, I think, obvious that as the information is collected it must be ordered in some way if it is to remain coherent and controllable. Using a card system (a 'notes on paper slips system' can be modified accordingly) the technique is to take a box of the correct size for the cards and divide it by means of cards of slightly larger size (or strips of cardboard) into sections, each bearing the name of one of the subject areas decided upon by the student. Ready-made card filing boxes are available from most stationery shops but if the subject matter requires the collection of masses of data empty shoe boxes make a most suitable substitute.

Once the card filing system is ready then, as the books and articles are read, the cards are completed – not forgetting to quote the source of the information – and can then be filed under the specific subject heading. In this way the information is collected in an organised fashion and on suitable occasions it is possible, by physical inspection, to ascertain in which areas the information is scanty or over-abundant.

If further subject areas are decided upon, the relevant divider card can be inserted and the cards subsequently accumulated by you can be assembled therein.

Those with some experience of this type of information accumulation will realise that this system goes some way towards dealing with two of the worst problems involved in this type of work. First, when reading a book or an article, the most difficult question is to decide what notes should be taken. In this case, if the information under consideration does not fit into any subject area division, a conscious decision to open up a new subject area must be made. This alone will usually give pause and avoid accumulating unnecessary information. Secondly, the dreadful horror-inspiring problem of masses of notes lying in bundles around your room will not occur. The cards can be filed as and when they are prepared. Of course mistakes will be made, and you will later need to transfer certain information to other subject divisions, but for the most part, the greater amount of the information will be categorised correctly. And, even if you find it necessary to transfer cards between subject area divisions, this is an easy procedure because only one item of information has been inserted on each card. You should note that cards will often need to be cross-referenced to other information cards, and for this purpose you will need to devise a simple system of numbering the cards.

Finally then comes the point at which it is necessary to consider drafting an outline of the essay. Well the position is not too bad if you have followed the procedure suggested above and the overall essay or research paper subject has been broken down into a number of smaller and manageable subject divisions.

Information has been collected on cards under specific subject areas and can be tackled piecemeal. By this time you should have a reasonable idea of the overall structure of the argument. The process of reading and note-taking has probably led to either confirmation or amendment of your original structure. You will be able to take out the information cards in each section (and since they are written in your own active vocabulary you will easily be able to understand them and absorb them) and to sift and re-arrange them in an order which will provide the basic facts and ideas needed for and relevant to each given section of your essay or research paper. You will discard some cards as no longer relevant – in fact, a good working basis is that one tends to use directly only about two-fifths of one's accumulated material.

On the other hand, throughout the period of material accumulation, you should similarly have written out, on fresh cards, ideas that have occurred to you, and inserted these cards into the appropriate sub-divisions of your material. The part which each subject section will play in the overall structure should now be pretty well clear. What remains is to think – and to write.

I shall attempt to deal in the next Section with the method which you, the student, should adopt in this stage of your work.

SECTION 2

WRITING IT OUT

2

WRITING IT OUT

Let us assume that you have some sort of rough structure; a list of subject areas and a fairly reasonable accumulation of data and references on cards within each of the subject areas. You have gone through the data cards in each subject area, have extracted irrelevant data and have put the cards into some form of order which relates to the progression of writing you intend to follow when dealing with that subject area. Each data card will be in the words of your active vocabulary (with a few exceptions) and you have a reasonably complete understanding of the data thereon.

A FIRST DRAFT

Now, in my view, although a few students, post-graduate or otherwise, are capable of putting together their theses or dissertations at the first attempt, those people are very much more the exception than the rule. I would recommend that a first draft, followed by one or more revised drafts, dependent on the time constraint, is an essential. The main evidence I would put forward to support this view is the difference in quality between the earlier and later parts of many theses or dissertations. Writing is a very difficult art – an art, I would suggest, to be learnt only by writing and writing and writing!

In many cases the student is called upon in his/her final year to produce a very large piece of written material – and writing may not often form an overlarge part of the student's curriculum. Invariably he/she starts off in a very halting fashion, which shows in the first parts of the thesis and by the time he/she has got to the point of writing the later parts of the thesis his/her creative writing ability has improved out of all recognition. But by this time it is often too late for him/her to go back and rewrite the earlier sections.

A first draft, therefore, I would argue, provides a great deal of valuable writing practice – practice, which is essential to acquiring the ability to write coherently, logically and even, perhaps, interestingly. But it also has other advantages. In a way, the art of writing out complicated material is most fascinating in that, although one may have a fairly well formed structure and conclusion, one is never quite sure what is actually going to emerge from the writing process. The art of writing, in my view, can be described as a fairly tight process of the structuring of one's thoughts – in a way in which the subconscious mind, sifting and ordering the material and data with which it has been inundated, is now, relatively suddenly, called upon to make a conscious and specific effort to create order out of this apparent chaos. Although the structure may have been tightly defined, although the data may have been discussed *ad nauseam*, it is still possible that, from the process of writing, new thought connections may be made and new thought patterns emerge which can, in some instances, totally alter the context and conclusion of the thesis. Writing, then, should be regarded as a dynamic process in the course of which many assumptions, inter-connections of data and previously-held conclusions may be questioned, reviewed and often totally revised.

The first draft also pulls together the data which was previously on cards and lessens the need for recall; if further information becomes available the written draft also offers a fairly stiff test of its relevance and, because the draft in effect represents a specific structure it can thus provide a guide to its point of insertion. However, one must be prepared to accept that new material can sometimes lead to the necessity of adjusting or restructuring the whole of the existing draft.

But apart from these advantages the main asset offered by a first draft is that it gives an opportunity to revise the text. It does this in two ways. First, it gives you an opportunity to circulate the draft text amongst your tutors with a view to gaining their expert comment on the draft as a whole and in its particular details. But, most important of all it gives you the opportunity to think again! Having written the first draft you should leave it alone for a few days and go on with some other work. When you return to it later you may well be amazed at the faults in structure and in detail that will leap to the eye as you examine it. Here I should perhaps add a note of apology to those students for whom it may well be the normal procedure to write up to five or six drafts before finalising the text of the thesis, and who will find it strange that I argue the case for a first draft at all.

However, before I turn to the details of writing the first draft, let me add that many individuals, when reading their own draft, suffer from what might be called 'word blindness'. By this I mean the inability to check one's own draft, in that the same error can be overlooked time and time again – mainly, I suspect, because the opening part of a sentence stimulates in the mind the remainder of the sentence and this reaction 'overpowers' the actual input through the optical and mental system. This inability to check the detail of one's own work can often be overcome by making an agreement with a colleague or fellow-student to check each other's work for this sort of detailed error. From my own

31

experience such an agreement, if carefully made (and honoured!), can be of great mutual advantage.

Finally, mention should be made of the advantage which a first draft offers in situations where one has, in the course of the research, to delve deeply into a subject area outside one's normal training and experience. In these circumstances one can take the results of this often brief and hasty foray into another discipline and having written them up one can present them to an expert in this strange field of study for his/her opinion. Thus one can often gain the reassurance that no great blunders have been made. This is a most useful technique for students whose studies may often require them to explore, briefly but efficiently, quite esoteric fields of inquiry.

THE 'INTRODUCTION' AND 'CONCLUSION'

There is no clear body of evidence to guide you, the student, in deciding at what point either the Introduction or the Conclusion should be written. If you feel that you have arrived at a fairly reasonable structure for the thesis, undoubtedly this is the time to sit down and write an Introduction, but let us be clear what the Introduction should contain.

In my view, the introductory section should:

a) State precisely the area of study. This is very important because you can hardly be criticised for failing to cover something outside the area of research you have defined!

b) Explain why the research is being carried out.

c) Draw attention to the originality and the conclusions.

d) Point to the inadequacy of the work so far carried out in this area of research.

e) Describe the methods of research.

f) State what special difficulties have been encountered.

Additional points that might be included in the Introduction are a description of the change in values, assumptions and views that have been experienced throughout the research and a reference to the time constraint under which the work was carried out.

Many would argue that the Introduction is the most important part of the thesis. It is in the Introduction that the examiners are introduced to your style of writing, your methods of thought, the problem you have identified and attempted to tackle and though, undoubtedly, the bulk of your work will be of immense influence on them, can one doubt that 'first impressions' will not be of great importance even to these very expert and experienced individuals? My own view is that if I argue that the main draft must be written and rewritten in the form of a first and second draft, then the Introduction must be rewritten and polished continually until it 'shines like a jewel'. The first draft of the Introduction should be attempted as soon as you feel that you have formulated a reasonable structure – in fact writing the Introduction can be used to test the structure – and then the Introduction should be continually rewritten as the research progresses.

The question of when to write the Conclusion is undoubtedly even more complex. The brief outline of possible, expected or anticipated conclusions, included in the introduction, is undoubtedly of great use in clarifying and defining the purpose of the research, but any attempt to arrive at these, in too great detail, evidently pre-supposes a knowledge of the conclusions before the research has been carried out, or smacks of an unscientific bias which is the antithesis of the purpose of research or study. My own view is that a clear distinction should be made at an early stage of the research between, on the one hand, the possible conclusions that may emerge or the hypotheses that are being tested, which must necessarily be delineated as a test of the structure, and, on the other hand, the actual research-based conclusions which can be written only when the research has actually been carried out. Finally, the Conclusion should also include an assessment of the soundness of the whole thesis, with perhaps suggestions of how further research in the same subject area might be carried forward. Do avoid, at all costs, any implied assumption that, with your thesis, you have rendered the whole subject no longer worth further exploration or that your solution has achieved the optimum.

PUTTING THE FACTS TOGETHER

Given that the student has a series of cards with references and quotations, the technique of putting these together is often misunderstood. On a fairly large number of occasions tutors are faced with a thesis consisting of a string of quotations or references with literally only a few words in between. Analogies are often very dangerous devices but if one uses the analogy of building a wall of argument with the bricks as the references and quotations and the cement as the individual's arguments, perhaps in this instance the analogy is not inappropriate. (Though even in this crude analogy the relative sizes of the bricks and the cement are very misleading). To re-emphasise the point, the facts, references, quotations that the student has unearthed must be used in *support* of the argument. What you have to do is to write out the structure of your argument, inserting appropriately the quotations and references to reinforce and hold up the structure of the argument. You must avoid simply listing the sources and quotations without adequate support.

References and quotations also serve a number of other purposes. They illustrate the depth and width of reading; they can enable subsequent researchers to pin-point exactly a specific reference (for this reason page/paragraph numbers must be given) and they enable the reader, to some extent, to assess the quality of the evidence used to support an argument. If this latter point is questioned (as it often is!) you should ask yourself, *ceteris paribus*, (all other things being equal) what assessment would be made of an argument used in an article if the source was given as either the milkman or, say, a well-known expert in the subject? However, in my view, the main purpose of references is that they enable the reader to differentiate clearly between, on the one hand, what may be YOUR opinion or argument, and, on the other hand, when you are quoting evidence in support of your argument. Providing you have clearly understood the preceding paragraph, you will find, I suggest that the correct use of quotations and references will enable you to structure each particular section of your essay, paper or thesis in a logical, analytical and, even perhaps, in an interesting way.

A further point on the use of quotations and references is that it should be clearly stated when they are being used and, in most instances, an opinion on their validity should be expressed. For example, let us suppose you write: 'there are five categories of causal factors' – and you have personally devised such a taxonomy, classification or arrangement you should make this clear, and be prepared to justify it!. If, however, you have obtained this from a book or article then you must state 'Jones (reference number) has put forward five categories' and then express an opinion on the validity and reliability of this taxonomy.

MISCELLANEOUS

For details of how to list references and quotations, a large number of books are commonly available in any library. Particular attention should be paid to the use of 'ibid.' and 'op. cit.' to deal with successive quotations or references from the same source. (But do note that there are alternative ways described by which the use of 'ibid.' and 'op. cit.' can be avoided).

The general trend today seems to be to use footnotes at the foot of the page of text only where they are essential to carry forward the argument or discussion and to place all other references and sources at the end of the section concerned. Do remember that a reference should enable the reader to locate the specific source or quotation and so it is usual to give: Author's name – Author's initials – Title of book or article – (place of publication, publisher, date of publication) – page or paragraph number(s).

Regarding quotations, note that it is customary to include four lines or less in the text within single quotation marks and to indent longer quotations (with single line spacing) without quotation marks.

Moreover, do ensure in the first draft that double or treble spacing is used with, in addition, large gaps left between paragraphs in order that adequate space is available for the insertion of subsequent ideas, amendments and suggestions. Of course, if you have access to a computer word-processing programme (particularly one with a spelling check and thesaurus system) and a database programme (for use with references) you will have no difficulty with subsequent changes and alterations to your initial draft.

Finally, when you actually start writing up your work, let me suggest that you follow the procedure, adopted by many experienced writers, of doing a set amount of writing every day. This can be in the form of so many hundred words or so many hours each day. Creative writing is a very demanding task and at all costs the idea that you can write for hours and hours, without marked deterioration in the quality of the style of writing, must be eradicated from your mind.

SECTION 3

THE STRUCTURED QUESTION TECHNIQUE

3

THE STRUCTURED QUESTION TECHNIQUE

In this section I propose to attempt to deal primarily with the choice of subject and how such a choice can be narrowed by study, analysis and testing.

The first point to be emphasised is that a clear distinction must be made between, on the one hand, the choice of the general area of research and, on the other hand, the decision about the final specific subject of investigation which will ultimately be represented in the title of the essay, thesis or dissertation.

Contrary to what many students believe, it is almost invariably impossible to select a specific title for a thesis or dissertation without having first carried out a great deal of groundwork and background research. The general area of research is usually not too difficult to select – indeed, in many cases it will be set by your tutor – and will represent, perhaps, a chance to explore in depth a question or problem that interests you and which you have not previously had the time or opportunity to investigate. It will also represent a particular interest or interests, stimulated by past discussion or reading, and it is important that you attempt to define these interests in your own mind as they will, in all probability, tend to provide the essential motivation in the period of arduous research that lies ahead of you.

Most students are aware, well in advance, that they will be required to select a subject for their dissertation or thesis and it is very important that some prior thought is given, as early as possible, to defining, and attempting to make explicit, possible general areas of study. Indeed it may well be worthwhile for institutional arrangements to be made for students to be given the opportunity to discuss such general areas of study well before the commencement of the formal period of research or study. However, when the general area of research has been selected a phase of narrowing and defining the subject must then take place. This phase varies with different educational institutions and may in some cases be as long as a year before the final thesis title must be selected and registered (this period may also include training in research theories and practice). You must make yourself acquainted with the rules concerned and be quite clear at which times you are required to put forward the general area of study you have selected and when you are required formally to state your final specific subject of research.

At this stage, perhaps, an example will assist. You may find that you are interested in studying the Second World War – and the set area of study allows such an interest to be pursued. As you carry out your initial period of investigation into the subject you find that the 1939-45 period of conflict is an enormous subject which you cannot possibly tackle. The area of study is then narrowed, perhaps, to the campaigns in North Africa and again as your research into the subject continues and the ramifications and complexities of the subject become apparent, especially in view of the lack of sources and the time constraint under which you must work, so the subject of investigation may narrow again down to the campaigns in Egypt and Libya; to the Eighth Army campaigns; to the campaigns of Alexander and Montgomery; to the supply problems in the last advance and, finally, to the psychological problems resulting from combat conditions. This simple example does, I trust, show that the process of narrowing the study or subject is clearly essential. You must be realistic and accept that what might take a trained team of researchers two or three years to complete cannot be undertaken by the most enthusiastic student in three or four weeks!

You must also be prepared to discover that your selected research topic has already been thoroughly investigated, or alternatively that the subject that you thought held great potential turns out to be of only trivial interest, providing little or no motivation. Accordingly it may often be worthwhile to have at this early stage a number of alternative areas of study in reserve – it may even be useful for a number of general areas of study to be submitted, with a priority of interest indicated, in order to cater for this type of situation.

Throughout this phase of moving from a general area of research towards a specific study title you will be carrying on a process of initial research. This phase will include preliminary readings around the subject – and here you are strongly recommended to become familiar with the layout of the library and with the services which it can provide. Time spent on discovering the relevant bibliographies, references and sources is never wasted, especially at this early stage. The importance of this phase of initial research cannot be overstressed, and indeed, it should, in some instances, precede even the selection of the general area of research or study! It is during this phase that you should attempt to gain an overview of the problem area and a knowledge of the central issue, existing theories and current views and hypotheses. There is also the vital need to ensure that you are at least aware of any work already carried out; clearly any research not based on a review of the relevant literature will invariably be fundamentally unsound.

You should also refer to the methods of acquiring the techniques of learning and how to read quickly and efficiently described earlier in Section 1. At the same time, you should be in contact with your tutor or tutors, who can not only provide advice and guidance on the suitability of your general area of research but can point out possible directions in which the narrowing process can take place; the problems involved (particularly in the methodology); and will be able to assist in the perennial problem of finding bibliographies and sources of relevant information. The difficulty, though, is of having a procedure or system available by which you can test the suitability, depth and inherent structure of the research or study area which you are attempting to investigate, at all the various stages of the process.

One such procedure is what might be called the 'structured question technique' (or SQT) which is, in effect, a variation on similar processes used in a number of other academic disciplines.

If you have carefully read Section 1, you will have seen described a system whereby a general essay or research question can be expanded and amplified by setting a series of questions which can then be used to provide alternative areas of study. These, in turn, can subsequently be co-ordinated and synthesised into a structure forming the basis of the study or essay. The structured question technique (or SQT) is an extension of this which can be applied to much more complicated research or advanced study topics.

The SQT proceeds in a series of stepped questions as follows:

PHASE A

You must ask yourself what is the basic fundamental question that your paper or thesis is proposing to answer. This is a difficult process and means that when someone reads the completed paper or thesis he/she will be able to say that such and such a question was asked and such and such an answer (or answers) was attempted in the thesis. This question is known as the MAIN QUESTION or the PHASE A question.

PHASE B

Having clarified the MAIN QUESTION, your next step is to ask what sub-questions must be posed and answered in order to answer the MAIN or PHASE A question. At this phase the questions asked are known as SUB-QUESTIONS or PHASE B questions.

PHASE C

The SQT continues by asking what sub-sub-questions must be posed and answered in order to answer the sub-questions or PHASE B questions. These sub-sub questions are known as the PHASE C questions.

By forcing you to formulate the outline of your research into a number of distinct, but related, series of questions in a structured question form the SQT enables you to think of the work you have to do as a series of smaller tasks or problems which can be tackled piecemeal.

You are also required by this technique to clarify what levels of enquiry you must undertake in order to form a logical progression and structure – a structure with no gaps or jumps in the arguments and methodology. The SQT can invariably be used to define the gaps in the structure of knowledge, enquiry and argument required to assemble and synthesise the required units of enquiry. It should be clearly understood that in applying the SQT it may well be that questions at the PHASE B or C level, for example, may need to be formulated before the PHASE A question may be attempted. Similarly questions at PHASE D or E may spring to mind and demonstrate the absence of a necessary question at PHASE C.

You are warned that the action of applying the SQT may well involve a painful mental process, for the system of turning what may well represent days and weeks of interesting discussion and reading into formulated questions of this sort is far from an easy one – worthwhile though it will inevitably prove to be. It should be clear that, after the initial research phase has been completed, the SQT can be usefully applied at any stage, indeed even at the very beginning of the narrowing process, referred to earlier in this section, of moving from a general area of study or research down to a specific essay, thesis or dissertation title.

SECTION 4

AIDS TO WRITING

4

AIDS TO WRITING

Often the most difficult part of writing is getting started, particularly if you have not been able to write up drafts of your notes as your collection of note cards has been accumulating. When you stare at a blank page or a blank computer screen, surrounded by your boxes of note cards, confused by questions of punctuation or grammar, unable to find the right words or phrases a feeling of helplessness, even panic, may set in. Well do not panic – and be comforted by the fact that even professional writers suffer the same experience time after time (creative writing never becomes easy!). This feeling is known as 'writer's block', but fortunately a number of techniques are available to help you overcome the fact that your writing process is stalled even before it has begun! But let us be clear – if you have not followed the advice given in the earlier sections and you have not put together a logical structure of questions, and have not accumulated a well-ordered set of notes and quotations, then you are in trouble. Unless you are very skilled at writing creatively with no real data or substance then I am afraid your writer's block will remain a permanent state.

OVERCOMING WRITER'S BLOCK

So let us assume that you do have a reasonable structure in your mind and adequate notes, references and quotations all neatly laid out on note cards and sub-divided and ordered according to the intended structure and yet you still cannot get started. Then, in that predicament, here are some practical techniques you can try.

1. Talk to a tape-recorder

Yes, I am serious – sit down at your desk, switch on your tape-recorder and talk to it. Usually as the recorder whirs away and you sit there silently you begin to feel so embarrassed that you will be forced into talking. Try to say in your own words what you are trying to write about, perhaps discuss the overall structure, or the particular section you are trying to write or even the particular paragraph or sentence you are actually trying to put together. The technique depends upon your using your active vocabulary (your everyday vocabulary) rather than the formal vocabulary needed for writing, as was outlined in Section 1. Frankly, it does not matter which aspect of your writing you discuss as long as you just talk and talk and talk! Frequently you will find that your thoughts are sorted out by this process – but, above all, using your active vocabulary will help to break up your writer's block. What then? Well, you rewind and play back the tape and listen to your own thoughts and words. Invariably you will find that by using your active vocabulary you have managed to state quite elegantly what particular thought or statement was in your mind. The much easier task is now to turn this active vocabulary into your formal vocabulary and get it down on paper. You may, at first, feel quite foolish talking to a tape-recorder, but try it, you may find that it works for you.

Would it not, you may ask, be better to talk to a friend or acquaintance instead of a tape-recorder? The answer here is that it depends... The trouble is that first, it's often very embarrassing to put into words a jumble of incoherent thoughts – for, in effect, your intellect is trying to make sense of a great mass of data and ideas. Secondly, you may find that your listener may tend to interrupt you with either questions or comments which may well disturb your train of thoughts; thirdly, you will have no record of the complex pattern of ideas and solutions that you have formulated and, finally, most disconcerting of all, the listener may suddenly say, 'I must start cooking the dinner' or worst of all, may fall fast asleep!

2. Regularise your writing habits

One concept that may be the cause of your writer's block is that you have been conditioned to 'waiting for inspiration to strike' when suddenly all your thoughts will clarify, the mantle of authorship will descend upon you and all your writing problems will disappear. Well, I am going to be bluntly rude and tell you to forget all that nonsense and accept that creative writing, though it is clearly an art, is invariably the product of perspiration, hard regular work, practised skill and – for those lucky ones – a touch of talent.

If you were ever to study the writing habits of many famous authors you would be astonished to find a pattern somewhat as follows. Each day, at a certain time, usually after breakfast, they retire to their study or room and do not emerge until they have completed a specific number of hours of work or, more likely, a specific number of words. That's it! The secret, if there is one, is that you have to force yourself into the habit of, say, at 9 o'clock each morning, sitting down at your desk or computer (possibly with your tape-recorder at the ready) and not leaving the room (except for obvious reasons) until you have completed, say, three hours of work or five hundred or a thousand words. The latter target of a set number of words is usually the better objective – you tell yourself that each day you will write, say, five hundred words and you will not leave the desk or computer until this set task is completed. If your ability or the stage of your thought is sufficiently advanced and you can set your objective at a thousand words per day – even better still. Think of it – one thousand words per day is five thousand per week (yes – keep the weekend free!) and this is twenty thousand per month!

You can even set yourself little rewards. If your daily task is five hundred words (about one and a half pages of writing) and you manage – for your thoughts are flowing well – say, eight hundred then the next day you will have only two hundred to write in order to maintain your average and can have an easier day. Of course, if you manage a thousand then you can have the next morning completely free.

Some creative writers, I know, work better in the evening or late at night and if you belong to this group then adjust your schedule accordingly. However, in my experience, too many distractions tend to intrude in evening work and if you *can* write in the morning, you are more likely to be fresh and alert. Of course, if you have to attend lectures, seminars and/or meetings. throughout the day you may well have to do your creative writing in the evening or at the weekends but the principle of establishing regular writing habits is the secret. Write for one hour each evening and three hours on Sunday, for example.

One further tip you might find useful is that when you are writing your set number of words you should, at this stage, look up specific references or quotations, but try to keep the flow of writing going. Just make a note that a reference, quotation or whatever, is required and when you have finished then look up the specific details you require to insert in your text.

3. Brainstorming

Four reasonably well-known brainstorming techniques are involved here and these have even been incorporated into word-processing/writing computer programmes like WORDBENCH. These include 'Freewriting' where you must try to force yourself to write for a selected period, five or ten minutes, without allowing yourself to look back at what you have written or even pausing in your writing. You can use this technique when speaking to your tape-recorder.

'Invisible Writing' requires the use of a computer or typewriter for it involves your blanking out with a piece of cardboard the screen or typewriter paper so that you cannot see what you have written. The idea is that you will not be distracted by what you have written and thus will be able to keep your ideas flowing!

'Nutshelling' encourages you to present the main purpose of your writing in a few carefully constructed phrases or sentences and 'Goal Setting' encourages you to state precisely your target audience, purpose and point of view in a few short sentences.

The mention of target audience is worth noting because it is a point you may tend to overlook. Professional writers spend a great deal of time identifying their target audience because, amongst other things, the amount of explanation necessary for a knowledgeable audience (such as your tutor/supervisor in the present context) is clearly different from that required for the general public.

Do think about your target audience – which may well be only your tutors – and bearing in mind their knowledge and expertise, write accordingly. With luck they may even find some new knowledge in what you have written and, best of all, they may even find it interesting!

WORD PROCESSING (additional facilities)

Over the past few years I have not seen any essay, paper, dissertation or thesis which has not been written on a word processor so there is good evidence to assume that usage of computers is now widespread.

What is surprising is most students' lack of knowledge of the many other facilities that are included in the better word-processing packages.

Let us examine some of these facilities and if you are about to buy a word-processing package it will give you some idea of the features you might require. The main writing facility is the spelling checker. Today nearly all word-processing programmes include a spelling checker though these can vary in size between 50,000 and 150,000 words. Most include the ability to add your own words either within a general or personal dictionary and often technical, legal or medical dictionaries can be purchased separately. I understand that dictionaries for foreign languages are also becoming available. Usually the spelling checker can be configured as memory resident which means it can be called into use anywhere in a document at any time or, alternatively, it can be installed and called up separately. It all depends on the capacity of your computer and whether you are running the programme on floppies or on a hard disc. Do bear in mind that the spelling checker checks only if a word exists in its dictionary and that it cannot determine whether you meant to write 'hear' instead of 'here' or 'collage' instead of 'college'. You may also find that it may have difficulty with apostrophes, words with numbers and plurals. If you can, try to ensure that you get a British rather than an American version otherwise you will find it tiresome having to change words like criticize and exercize to criticise and exercise and labor to labour. Spelling checkers can usually be used to check one word, part of a document or the whole of a document, and many include a word-count facility.

A few programmes now include a thesaurus which by providing a list of alternative words can immeasurably enhance a piece of writing. Where students have to make reference to other authors it is common to read that so and so 'states' repeated endlessly in page after page. Reference to the thesaurus in a word-processing package will provide alternatives like 'comments, argues, contends, points out, advises, imparts' – the list is almost endless – and all these are available in a few seconds!

Antonyms, or opposites in meaning, are also available in some programmes and some of them even provide word definitions. The way to use the thesaurus is to place the cursor on the word for which alternatives are required and to press the appropriate key – as simple as that.

Perhaps the writing facility that comes next in importance is the Outliner. In the earlier Section 1, I have argued that no matter the size or complexity of the work it is essential to create a structure by listing relevant headings (or questions) and sub-headings (or sub-questions) which can then be moved and reorganised as the overall pattern of the work becomes clearer. The Outliner programme provides this facility – for the headings and sub-headings can be expanded, amended, moved or even hidden as required. Detailed notes or preliminary thoughts can be 'hung on' to each heading or sub-heading and can then be moved as the initial headings are reorganised until the final structure emerges. The most obvious example would be if you were planning the structure of a book, for the Table of Contents would represent the list of ordered headings and the description of the contents of each chapter would be the sub-headings and notes. You will find that learning to use an Outliner in a word-processing programme does require a determined effort but I have found that once the principles and relevant key strokes are grasped it's difficult to understand how one ever managed without it.

The Search and Replace facility contained in many word-processing programmes can also be useful. Essentially this allows you to instruct the programme to search for a word or phrase of your choice. All sorts of interesting variations are available. Let us say that you have written a long history paper and found that the date of 1237 you had used should have read 1238. Simply instruct the programme to search for the incorrect date or text and either automatically, or at your specific request, as each entry is found, to correct the error. The whole document can be amended in a few seconds!.

Another important writing facility involves what are usually called Block commands. Whenever you want to move or copy a block of text, either within your current working document or to and from another document or save or print that specific piece of text then this is available by the Block command. I cannot over-emphasise how extremely useful this facility can be. I tend to use it when I find that a specific and long paragraph is in the wrong location within my current Outliner structure or when I need to transcribe a long detailed quotation between documents. Technical writers will appreciate, I am sure, how time-saving it can be to be able to avoid transcription errors with a 100% accuracy. Some word processing systems have a 'windows' facility which enables you to view two windows of different texts on the screen – you can edit text in either window by switching (activating) between the windows – and then to block text between the two windows is a simple and viewable procedure. Using the block system consists simply of marking the beginning and end of the text to be moved and then marking where the block is to be inserted within the document and finally pressing the appropriate keys. It's easier still if your word-processing system incorporates the use of a mouse – for then the marking and destination point is actually perceivable on the screen as well as being a great deal faster.

If you have, from time to time, to prepare long complex documents or reports a whole further series of writing tools are available to assist you in a number of word-processing programmes. These tools include the generating of a Table of Contents, tables of authorities and automatic cross-referencing within a text, automatic paragraph-numbering and index-creation. What many writers will find particularly useful is the fact that automatic cross-referencing can encompass page numbers, section numbers and even footnote numbers. What is still needed is some form of automatic sensing so that when you move a reference, 'above' can become 'below', but I have no doubt that this will soon be available.

Turning to indexing, if you have ever had to undertake the monumental task of preparing an index for your book or paper you will know that there are few jobs more boring or tiresome. With the proper word-processing programme the task becomes reduced to marking the words and phrases (and sub-headings if required) that you want included in the index and then the programme will produce the required list. The first time you use indexing you may well find it rather tricky but, in principle, you should not find it too difficult. A number of variations of style and layout are possible including the capability of inserting in the index words or phrases which do not appear in the body of the document.

In connection with professional writing reference must be made to specialist writing packages (WORDBENCH, a relatively inexpensive package – about £100 – is a good example) which are specifically devoted to meeting the needs of students. Perhaps Wordbench's most novel tool is its provision of the four 'brainstorming' techniques to help overcome 'writer's block', referred to earlier in this Section.

Dedicated writing programmes like Wordbench provide a whole series of inter-connected facilities based on the premise that all the different parts of a document, book, paper or thesis are related to one another within an overall structure. Thus Wordbench provides an Outliner, a Notetaker, which allows notes to be gathered in the form of what might be called electronic notecards, and these can be assigned to specific Outliner headings and sub-headings; and a Reference Tool for entering and recording references to specific notecards can be created in the Notetaker. All these are then gathered together in a Folder in the form of a normal word-processing document, the Writer, as a first draft for editing. A Spelling checker and thesaurus programme is then available as well as a Viewer (a split-screen programme), a Format tool (for enhancing and formatting the document), a Print Manager (for automatically generating tables of contents, bibliographies, footnotes and so on.) and the Add-In Manager, which includes the brainstorming techniques described earlier.

Of particular interest if you are involved in writing which requires complex references and bibliographies is the Reference Tool which gives invaluable advice on the vexed problem of how, and in what form, references should be listed and entered. Do you know how to refer to a book by a deceased author which has been published under a new title? As a word-processing package, however, many of the features of the more expensive packages are missing. Wordbench is available for the PC and Apple but not yet for the Macintosh but I think we shall soon see all of its tools incorporated in the top range of word-processing packages.

This brief review of the main writing techniques in many word-processing packages has, I trust, given you some idea of the writing facilities that are available to help you and increase your efficiency. In my experience it is not necessary to try to learn all of them – the key point is to know that they exist and what they can do and then turn to them as and when your work requires it.

'It is important that students bring a certain ragamuffin, barefoot irreverence to their studies; they are not here to worship what is known but to question it.'

J. Bronowski, *The Ascent of Man*
(London, B.B.C. 1973) p.360

Other titles by the author:

Newman, Roland J. *The Road and Christ Church Meadow*. Oxford, Bookmarque, 1988.

SELECTED REFERENCES

All Polytechnic, University and College libraries will have a wide selection of publications relevant to research generally and your discipline specifically.

The following three publications have been selected as being particularly relevant to the approach outlined in this book. In addition, all three of these publications themselves contain a list of references which can provide you with further guidance if required.

Leedy, Paul D. *Practical Research: Planning and Design*. 2nd ed. London, Collier Macmillan, 1980.

Turabian, Kate L. *A Manual for Writers of Term Papers, Theses and Dissertations*. 5th ed. Chicago, U. of Chicago Press, 1987.

Van Dalen, D.B. *Understanding Educational Research*. 4th ed. London, McGraw-Hill, 1979.